SCIENCE KIDS
Colors

BLUE

Jared Siemens

LET'S READ
AV2 BY WEIGL
ADDED VALUE • AUDIO VISUAL

www.av2books.com

LET'S READ

AV²
BY WEIGL™

ADDED VALUE • AUDIO VISUAL

Go to **www.av2books.com**, and enter this book's unique code.

BOOK CODE

H465741

AV² by Weigl brings you media enhanced books that support active learning.

AV² provides enriched content that supplements and complements this book. Weigl's AV² books strive to create inspired learning and engage young minds in a total learning experience.

Your AV² Media Enhanced books come alive with...

Audio
Listen to sections of the book read aloud.

Video
Watch informative video clips.

Embedded Weblinks
Gain additional information for research.

Try This!
Complete activities and hands-on experiments.

Key Words
Study vocabulary, and complete a matching word activity.

Quizzes
Test your knowledge.

Slide Show
View images and captions, and prepare a presentation.

... and much, much more!

Published by AV² by Weigl
350 5th Avenue, 59th Floor New York, NY 10118
Websites: www.av2books.com   www.weigl.com

Library of Congress Control Number: 2014934867

ISBN 978-1-4896-1246-5 (hardcover)
ISBN 978-1-4896-1247-2 (softcover)
ISBN 978-1-4896-1248-9 (single user eBook)
ISBN 978-1-4896-1249-6 (multi-user eBook)

Printed in the United States of America in North Mankato, Minnesota
1 2 3 4 5 6 7 8 9 0 18 17 16 15 14

042014
WEP150314

Project Coordinator: Aaron Carr
Designer: Mandy Christiansen

Weigl acknowledges Getty Images and iStock as the primary image suppliers for this title.

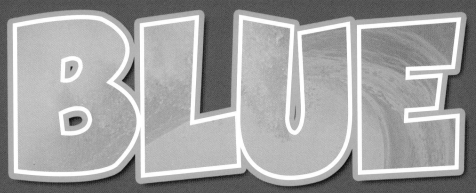

CONTENTS

2   AV² Book Code

4   What Is Blue?

6   Blue at Home

8   Blue Food

10   Blue Toys

12   Blue Outside

14   Blue Animals

16   Blue on the Playground

18   Blue at School

20   What Blue Means

22   Sort It Out

24   Key Words/AV2books.com

What is this color?
I like it the best.

I like the color blue
more than the rest.

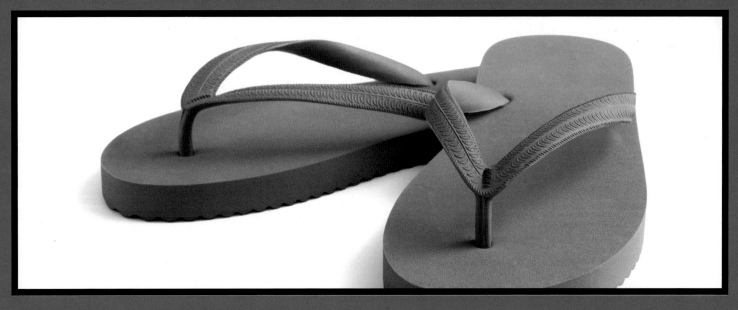

In the bathroom I found
a blue toothbrush and comb.

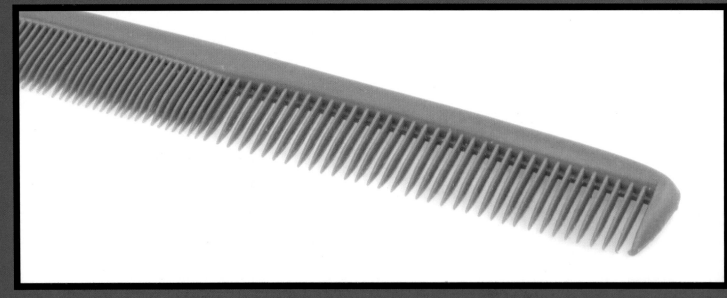

What other blue things can be found in your home?

7

I see
a blue lollipop.

I see
a blue treat.

Are there any blue foods that are healthy to eat?

I see
a blue duck.

I see
a blue car.

Count how many
blue toys there are.

There is blue
in the sky.

There is blue
in the sea.

Is there more blue outside?
What do you see?

I see
a blue fish.

I see
a butterfly, too!

How many blue animals
live at the zoo?

I see
blue slides.

I see
blue swings.

I see blue at the playground.
There are many blue things.

I see
a blue locker.

I see
a blue chair.

Are there blue things at school?
Please tell me where.

Blue can mean wet.

Blue can mean cold.

What kind of things does this blue bin hold?

Find where these blue things belong in this book.

Go back through the pages and have a close look!

KEY WORDS

Research has shown that as much as 65 percent of all written material published in English is made up of 300 words. These 300 words cannot be taught using pictures or learned by sounding them out. They must be recognized by sight. This book contains 55 common sight words to help young readers improve their reading fluency and comprehension. This book also teaches young readers several important content words, such as proper nouns. These words are paired with pictures to aid in learning and improve understanding.

Page	Sight Words First Appearance	Page	Content Words First Appearance
4	I, is, it, like, the, this, what	4	color
5	more, than	5	blue
6	a, and, found, in	6	bathroom, comb, toothbrush
7	be, can, home, other, things, your	8	lollipop, treat
8	see	10	duck
9	any, are, eat, foods, that, there, to	11	toys
10	car	12	sky
11	how, many	13	outside
12	sea	14	butterfly, fish
13	do, you	15	zoo
14	too	16	slides, swings
15	animals, at, live	17	playground
19	me, school, tell, where	18	chair, locker
20	mean	20	cold, wet
21	does, kind, of	21	bin
22	book, find, these		
23	back, close, go, have, look, pages, through